# Loom Knit SAMPLERS

Lo...
It's easy when you ... any gauge loom and its appropriate yarn weight. Choose from 35 pattern stitches and three sampler options or create your own arrangement.

LEISURE ARTS, INC. • Maumelle, Arkansas

# LOOM KNIT SAMPLERS

Sampler afghans are easy to knit in strips and then sew together. Instructions for three blankets are included, as well as the option to use the pattern stitches of your choice. You can arrange the pattern stitches in different ways.

### Arrangement #1

As in the **lap-ghan**, you can make five strips, each in a different pattern stitch. The strips don't need to be the same width, but must be the same length.

### Arrangement #2

The **baby-ghan** is worked in four strips of equal width that make up the length of the blanket. Each strip is made up of three different pattern stitches, also worked in a different color.

### Arrangement #3

The width of the strips in the **afghan** form the length of the afghan. Each strip is made up of two or three different pattern stitches. Cable panels are ideal to use in this arrangement.

## Arrangement #1

| Strip 1 | Strip 2 | Strip 3 | Strip 4 | Strip 5 |
|---------|---------|---------|---------|---------|
|         |         |         |         |         |

## Arrangement #2

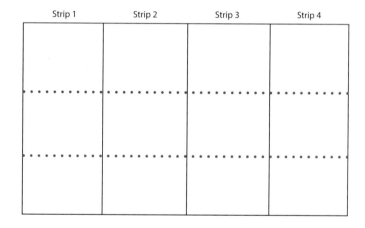

## Arrangement #3

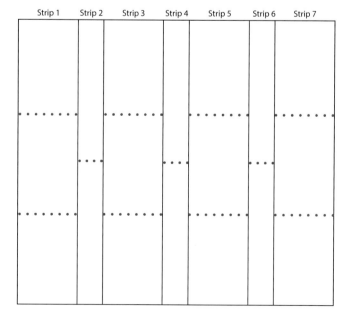

↑ **Working direction of all 3 arrangements**

# PLAN YOUR SAMPLER

**1. Choose the yarn.** Smooth yarns in colors that are not too dark will showcase the pattern stitches the best. Light weight yarn (#3) up to a super bulky weight yarn (#6) can be used. The weight of your yarn determines the size loom needed.

**2. Choose a loom to match your yarn weight.** The spacing of the pegs on the loom determines the loom gauge. The distance is measured from the center of one peg to the center of the next peg. The following chart is a guide to weights of yarn that work the best.

| Loom Gauge | Peg Spacing | Yarn Weight |
|---|---|---|
| Regular | ½" to ⁹⁄₁₆" 1.27 to 1.5 cm | #3 & #4 |
| Large | ⅝" to ¹¹⁄₁₆" 1.6 to 1.75 cm | #4 & #5 |
| Extra Large | ¾" to ¹⁵⁄₁₆" 1.9 to 2.4 cm | #5 & #6 |

**3. Make a stockinette stitch gauge swatch** using your chosen yarn and loom (knit every row). This will work for most of the pattern stitches made up of knit and purl stitches. The cable panels will be slightly smaller.

**4. Decide what size you want to make.** There is no "must" on the size. The following is a guideline of approximate sizes.
**Baby-ghan:** 34" x 45"
   (86.5 cm x 114.5 cm)
**Lap-ghan:** 36" x 48"
   (91.5 cm x 122 cm)
**Afghan:** 49" x 65"
   (124.5 cm x 165 cm)

**5. Decide on the orientation of the strips.** If working Arrangement #1, the stitches per inch will decide the width, and the rows per inch will decide the length. It's the opposite if working Arrangements #2 and #3. Worksheets are provided on pages 29-31.

**6. Now it's time for math.** Take the number of stitches per inch (2.54 cm) in your swatch and multiply it by the total number of inches you want for your overall finished width. Then decide how many strips you plan to use, and add one stitch for each edge that will be woven together (because the seams will use up one stitch at each edge).

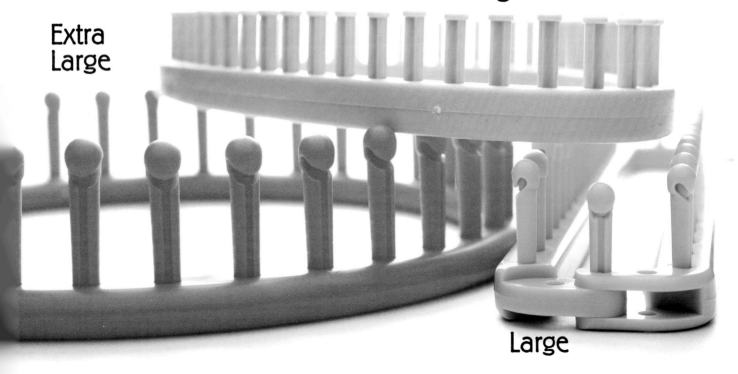

Extra Large

Regular

Large

*For example, if you want a finished measurement of 49" (124.5 cm) wide and your stitches per inch (2.54 cm) equal 2, then multiply 2 x 49 to get 98.*

*If you want 5 strips, add 8 stitches (1 each for the two end strips and 2 each for the center strips). This makes 106 stitches (pegs).*

The strips can be different widths, as long as they add up to the total number of stitches. If you want strips of equal widths, take the total number of stitches (106) and divide by the number of strips (5); this will reveal the average number of stitches (pegs) needed for each strip (21).

In some cases, that will not be the final number per strip. You may pick pattern stitches with multiples needing a few more stitches or a few less per strip. Also the total width of the finished project may end up being a little more or a little less than 49" (124.5 cm). But this formula will put you on the path to choosing pattern stitches.

The length of your afghan will be worked to any measurement you want, so no math is needed. Just be sure that all your strips are the same length.

**7. Choose the pattern stitches.** Keep in mind how many stitches you want each strip to have. You can have a few more or less stitches without greatly changing the finished size. Also, the cable panels won't be as wide as the panel with the same number of stitches worked in Stockinette Stitch.

The **multiple** is given for each of the pattern stitches. It is the number of pegs required to form one full repeat plus the number of pegs needed to work the pattern.

If you are planning a strip with more than one pattern stitch, the multiple can be different for each pattern as long as the **total** number of stitches (pegs) needed for each is the same.

*For example, if you want the strip to be 21 stitches (pegs), you can use a pattern stitch with a multiple of 4 + 1, 6 + 3, or any odd number.*

*The 21 stitches is just an approximate number. If the pattern stitch you want to use works better on 20 stitches, that is fine, too.*

You can always add edge stitches if you need 2 more stitches to add up to the needed number.

As mentioned, the strips do not all have to be the same width. Varying the size works as shown in the full-size afghan. So you might have one strip that uses 20 pegs, one strip that uses 14, one that uses 16, one that uses 32, etc. Just make the total number of stitches (pegs) of the strips equal the approximate number needed. But please remember, there are no "rules" when planning your sampler afghan.

Well, there is one rule:

**8. The length of the strips must measure the same.** It is easier to sew the strips together if all of the strips have the same number of rows. That may mean stopping in the middle of a stitch pattern. If the total is off by only one or two rows, the difference can simply be eased into the seam.

A good example is the sampler baby-ghan. Each block lines up because each pattern stitch uses exactly the same number of rows. To find this number, you would use the same formula above (for the number of stitches) but substitute the number of rows per inch (2.54 cm).

# LAP-GHAN

**Finished Size:** 35½" x 48" (90 cm x 122 cm)

■■□□▷ **EASY**

## · · · · · · · · SHOPPING LIST · · · · ·

**Yarn** (Medium Weight)

[4 ounces, 200 yards
(113 grams, 183 meters) per skein]:

☐  6 skeins

**Loom** (straight, large gauge)

☐  50 Pegs

## Additional Supplies

☐  Knitting loom tool

☐  Crochet hook, size K (6.5 mm)

☐  Yarn needle

## GAUGE INFORMATION

In Stockinette Stitch (knit every row),
   15 stitches and 22 rows = 4"
   (10 cm)

This lap-ghan is made of 5 strips.
Each strip is worked in a different
pattern stitch as indicated on the
placement diagram on page 6.

## STRIP 1

Working on the **inside** of the loom
from **right** to **left**, chain cast on
27 pegs; work as flat knitting.

Work #1 Granite Stitch, page 16, until
Strip measures 48" (122 cm) from
cast on edge.

Work chain one bind off across.

## STRIP 2

Working on the **inside** of the loom
from **right** to **left**, chain cast on
20 pegs; work as flat knitting.

Work #2 Double Garter Rib, page 16,
until Strip measures 48" (122 cm)
from cast on edge.

Work chain one bind off across.

## STRIP 3

Working on the **inside** of the loom from **right** to **left**, chain cast on 46 pegs; work as flat knitting.

Work #3 Basket Stitch, page 16, until Strip measures 48" (122 cm) from cast on edge.

Work chain one bind off across.

## STRIP 4

Working on the **inside** of the loom from **right** to **left**, chain cast on 21 pegs; work as flat knitting.

Work #4 Garter Rib 1 x 2, page 17, until Strip measures 48" (122 cm) from cast on edge.

Work chain one bind off across.

## STRIP 5

Working on the **inside** of the loom from **right** to **left**, chain cast on 27 pegs; work as flat knitting.

Work #5 Seersucker Stitch, page 17, until Strip measures 48" (122 cm) from cast on edge.

Work chain one bind off across.

## ASSEMBLY

Using Placement Diagram as a guide, weave Strips together *(Fig. 1, page 28)*.

**PLACEMENT DIAGRAM**

| Strip 1 | Strip 2 | Strip 3 | Strip 4 | Strip 5 |
|---|---|---|---|---|
| #1 Granite Stitch | #2 Double Garter Rib | #3 Basket Stitch | #4 Garter Rib 1 x 2 | #5 Seersucker Stitch |

↑ **Working direction**

# BABY-GHAN

**Finished Size:** 28" x 41" (71 cm x 104 cm)

 EASY

**Yarn** (Light Weight)

[3.5 ounces, 326 yards
(100 grams, 298 meters) per skein]:
- ☐ Grey - 2 skeins
- ☐ White - 2 skeins

**Loom** (oval, regular gauge)
- ☐ 54 Pegs

## Additional Supplies
- ☐ Knitting loom tool
- ☐ Crochet hook, size H (5 mm)
- ☐ Yarn needle

## GAUGE INFORMATION

In Stockinette Stitch (knit every row),
16 stitches and 24 rows =
4" (10 cm)

This baby-ghan is made of 4 strips.
Each strip is worked in 3 different
pattern stitches as indicated on the
placement diagram on page 10.
Colors are changed when each
pattern stitch is changed.

For easier assembly, work the same
number of rows for each pattern
stitch.

## STRIP 1

Working on the **inside** of the loom
from **right** to **left**, with White, chain
cast on 41 pegs; work as flat knitting.

Work #6 Andalusian Stitch, page 17,
until Strip measures 9" (23 cm) from
cast on edge, ending by working a
left to right row; cut White.

Using Grey, work #7 Squares Stitch,
page 17, until Strip measures 18"
(45.5 cm) from cast on edge, ending
by working a left to right row; cut
Grey.

Using White, work #8 Alternating
Andalusian Stitch, page 18, until Strip
measures 27" (68.5 cm) from cast on
edge.

Work chain one bind off across.

## STRIP 2

Working on the **inside** of the loom
from **right** to **left**, with Grey, chain
cast on 45 pegs; work as flat knitting.

Work #9 Double Basketweave,
page 18, until Strip measures 9"
(23 cm) from cast on edge, ending by
working a left to right row; cut Grey.

Using White, work #10 Checks Stitch,
page 18, until Strip measures 18"
(45.5 cm) from cast on edge, ending
by working a left to right row; cut
White.

Using Grey, work #11 Harris Tweed
Rib, page 18, until Strip measures 27"
(68.5 cm) from cast on edge.

Work chain one bind off across.

## STRIP 3

Working on the **inside** of the loom from **right** to **left**, with White, chain cast on 37 pegs; work as flat knitting.

Work #12 Seed Stitch Checks, page 19, until Strip measures 9" (23 cm) from cast on edge, ending by working a left to right row; cut White.

Using Grey, work #13 Grid Stitch, page 19, until Strip measures 18" (45.5 cm) from cast on edge, ending by working a left to right row; cut Grey.

Using White, work #14 Strokes Stitch, page 19, until Strip measures 27" (68.5 cm) from cast on edge.

Work chain one bind off across.

## STRIP 4

Working on the **inside** of the loom from **right** to **left**, with Grey, chain cast on 44 pegs; work as flat knitting.

Work #15 Woven Stitch, page 20, until Strip measures 9" (23 cm) from cast on edge, ending by working a left to right row; cut Grey.

Using White, work #16 Moss Stitch Checkers, page 20, until Strip measures 18" (45.5 cm) from cast on edge, ending by working a left to right row; cut White.

Using Grey, work #17 Staggered Interrupted Rib, page 20, until Strip measures 27" (68.5 cm) from cast on edge.

Work chain one bind off across.

## ASSEMBLY

Using Placement Diagram as a guide, weave Strips together *(Fig. 1, page 28)*.

## ATTACHED I-CORD EDGING

Using Grey, working across the loom to your left, and wrapping each peg counter-clockwise, e-wrap cast on 4 pegs.

Bring the baby-ghan into the center of the loom with the **right** side facing the pegs. Pick up a stitch by inserting the crochet hook through any stitch along the edge from **front** to **back** *(Fig. A)*. Catching the working yarn with the hook, bring it back through the knitting *(Fig. B)*. Twist the loop and place it on the next empty peg *(Fig. C)*.

★ Do **not** work back in the other direction. Instead, bring the working yarn along the inside of the loom, to the first peg that was worked. Knit or e-wrap knit the pegs in the same direction as the previous row *(Fig. D)*.

**PLACEMENT DIAGRAM**

| Strip 1 | Strip 2 | Strip 3 | Strip 4 |
|---|---|---|---|
| #8 Alternating Andalusian Stitch | #11 Harris Tweed Rib | #14 Strokes Stitch | #17 Staggered Interrupted Rib |
| #7 Squares Stitch | #10 Checks Stitch | #13 Grid Stitch | #16 Moss Stitch Checkers |
| #6 Andalusian Stitch | #9 Double Basketweave | #12 Seed Stitch Checks | #15 Woven Stitch |

↑ **Working direction**

Pick up a stitch in the next stitch of the piece; twist the loop and place it on the last peg that has a stitch. Knit it by lifting the bottom loop over the top loop and off the peg.

Repeat from ★ around the piece picking up a stitch in every stitch along the top and the bottom of the piece and in every other row along the sides. When rounding the corners of the piece, pick up an extra stitch in each of the corner stitches.

When you reach the starting point, work chain one bind off.

Sew the ends of the Edging together.

**Fig. A**

**Fig. B**

**Fig. C**

**Fig. D**

# AFGHAN

**Finished Size:** 49½" x 66" (125.5 cm x 167.5 cm)

 INTERMEDIATE

## ······· SHOPPING LIST ····

**Yarn** (Super Bulky Weight) **6**

[6 ounces, 106 yards

(170 grams, 97 meters) per skein]:

☐ 14 skeins

**Loom** (round, extra large gauge)

☐ 36 Pegs

### Additional Supplies

☐ Knitting loom tool

☐ Crochet hook, size K (6.5 mm)

☐ Yarn needle

## GAUGE INFORMATION

In Stockinette Stitch (knit every row),
8 stitches and 14 rows = 4" (10 cm)

This afghan is made of 7 strips.
Four strips are each worked in
3 different pattern stitches as
indicated on the placement diagram
on page 15. Three strips are each
worked in 2 different cable panels.

## STRIP 1

Working on the **inside** of the loom
from **right** to **left**, chain cast on
33 pegs; work as flat knitting.

Work #18 Moss Rib, page 21, until
Strip measures 16½" (42 cm) from
cast on edge, ending by working a
left to right row.

Work #19 Fleck Stitch, page 21, until
Strip measures 33" (84 cm) from cast
on edge, ending by working a left to
right row.

Work #20 Seeded Rib, page 21, until
Strip measures 49½" (125.5 cm) from
cast on edge, ending by working a
left to right row.

Work chain one bind off across.

## STRIP 2

Working on the **inside** of the loom
from **right** to **left**, chain cast on
14 pegs; work as flat knitting.

Work #30 Corkscrew Cable, page 25,
until Strip measures 24¾" (63 cm)
from cast on edge, ending by
working a left to right row.

Work #31 Elongated Wave Cable,
page 25, until Strip measures 49½"
(125.5 cm) from cast on edge, ending
by working a left to right row.

Work chain one bind off across.

## STRIP 3

Working on the **inside** of the loom
from **right** to **left**, chain cast on
26 pegs; work as flat knitting.

Work #21 Diagonal 4 Left, page 21,
until Strip measures 16½" (42 cm)
from cast on edge, ending by
working a left to right row.

Work #22 Fences Stitch, page 22,
until Strip measures 33" (84 cm) from
cast on edge, ending by working a
left to right row.

Work #23 Diagonal 4 Right, page 22, until Strip measures 49½" (125.5 cm) from cast on edge, ending by working a left to right row.

Work chain one bind off across.

## STRIP 4

Working on the **inside** of the loom from **right** to **left**, chain cast on 20 pegs; work as flat knitting.

Work #33 Double Cable Downwards, page 27, until Strip measures 24¾" (63 cm) from cast on edge, ending by working a left to right row.

Work #34 Double Cable Upwards, page 27, until Strip measures 49½" (125.5 cm) from cast on edge, ending by working a left to right row.

Work chain one bind off across.

## STRIP 5

Working on the **inside** of the loom from **right** to **left**, chain cast on 21 pegs; work as flat knitting.

Work #24 Double Andalusian Stitch, page 22, until Strip measures 16½" (42 cm) from cast on edge, ending by working a left to right row.

Work #25 Nubby Pattern, page 22, until Strip measures 33" (84 cm) from cast on edge, ending by working a left to right row.

Work #26 Interrupted Rib, page 23, until Strip measures 49½" (125.5 cm) from cast on edge, ending by working a left to right row.

Work chain one bind off across.

## STRIP 6

Working on the **inside** of the loom from **right** to **left**, chain cast on 16 pegs; work as flat knitting.

Work #32 Links Cable, page 25, until Strip measures 24¾" (63 cm) from cast on edge, ending by working a left to right row.

Work #35 Slipped Double Chain, page 27, until Strip measures 49½" (125.5 cm) from cast on edge, ending by working a left to right row.

Work chain one bind off across.

## STRIP 7

Working on the **inside** of the loom from **right** to **left**, chain cast on 32 pegs; work as flat knitting.

Work #27 Little Boxes, page 23, until Strip measures 16½" (42 cm) from cast on edge, ending by working a left to right row.

Work #28 Double Moss Stitch, page 23, until Strip measures 33" (84 cm) from cast on edge, ending by working a left to right row.

Work #29 Rectangular Checks, page 23, until Strip measures 49½" (125.5 cm) from cast on edge, ending by working a left to right row.

Work chain one bind off across.

## ASSEMBLY

Using Placement Diagram as a guide, weave Strips together *(Fig. 1, page 28)*.

### PLACEMENT DIAGRAM

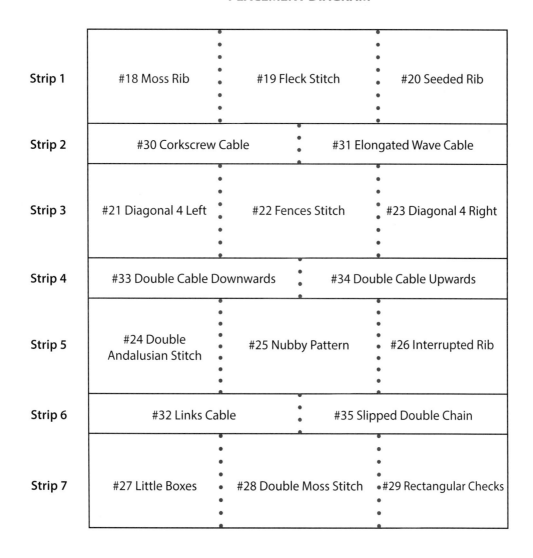

| | | | |
|---|---|---|---|
| Strip 1 | #18 Moss Rib | #19 Fleck Stitch | #20 Seeded Rib |
| Strip 2 | #30 Corkscrew Cable | #31 Elongated Wave Cable | |
| Strip 3 | #21 Diagonal 4 Left | #22 Fences Stitch | #23 Diagonal 4 Right |
| Strip 4 | #33 Double Cable Downwards | #34 Double Cable Upwards | |
| Strip 5 | #24 Double Andalusian Stitch | #25 Nubby Pattern | #26 Interrupted Rib |
| Strip 6 | #32 Links Cable | #35 Slipped Double Chain | |
| Strip 7 | #27 Little Boxes | #28 Double Moss Stitch | #29 Rectangular Checks |

→ **Working direction**

# Pattern Stitches

### #1 GRANITE STITCH

**Multiple:** odd number of pegs

**Rows 1 and 2:** Knit across.

**Rows 3 and 4:** K1, (P1, K1) across.

**Rows 5 and 6:** Knit across.

**Rows 7 and 8:** K2, P1, (K1, P1) across to last 2 pegs, K2.

Repeat Rows 1-8 for pattern.

### #2 DOUBLE GARTER RIB

**Multiple:** 4 pegs

**Row 1:** Knit across.

**Row 2:** K3, P2, (K2, P2) across to last 3 pegs, K3.

Repeat Rows 1 and 2 for pattern.

### #3 BASKET STITCH

**Multiple:** 6 + 4 pegs

**Rows 1 and 2:** Knit across.

**Rows 3-6:** K3, P4, (K2, P4) across to last 3 pegs, K3.

**Rows 7 and 8:** Knit across.

**Rows 9-12:** K1, P3, K2, (P4, K2) across to last 4 pegs, P3, K1.

Repeat Rows 1-12 for pattern.

## #4 GARTER RIB 1 x 2

**Multiple:** 3 pegs

**Row 1:** Knit across.

**Row 2:** K2, P2, (K1, P2) across to last 2 pegs, K2.

Repeat Rows 1 and 2 for pattern.

## #5 SEERSUCKER STITCH

**Multiple:** 4 + 3 pegs

**Rows 1 and 2:** K2, P1, (K1, P1) across to last 2 pegs, K2.

**Rows 3 and 4:** K1, P1, (K3, P1) across to last peg, K1.

**Rows 5 and 6:** K2, P1, (K1, P1) across to last 2 pegs, K2.

**Rows 7 and 8:** K3, (P1, K3) across.

Repeat Rows 1-8 for pattern.

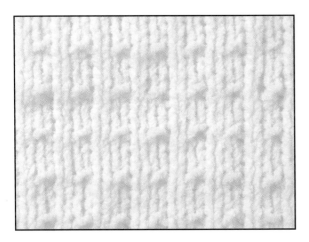

## #6 ANDALUSIAN STITCH

**Multiple:** odd number of pegs

**Rows 1-3:** Knit across.

**Row 4:** K2, P1, (K1, P1) across to last 2 pegs, K2.

Repeat Rows 1-4 for pattern.

## #7 SQUARES STITCH

**Multiple:** 5 + 1 pegs

**Row 1:** Knit across.

**Row 2:** K5, P1, (K4, P1) across to last 5 pegs, K5.

**Rows 3 and 4:** Repeat Rows 1 and 2.

**Row 5:** Knit across.

**Row 6:** K1, purl across to last peg, K1.

Repeat Rows 1-6 for pattern.

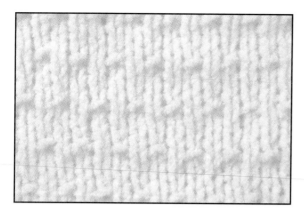

## #8 ALTERNATING ANDALUSIAN STITCH

**Multiple:** odd number of pegs

**Rows 1-3:** Knit across.

**Row 4:** K1, (P1, K1) across.

**Rows 5-7:** Knit across.

**Row 8:** K2, P1, (K1, P1) across to last 2 pegs, K2.

Repeat Rows 1-8 for pattern.

## #9 DOUBLE BASKETWEAVE

**Multiple:** 4 + 1 pegs

**Row 1:** Knit across.

**Row 2:** K1, (P3, K1) across.

**Rows 3 and 4:** Repeat Rows 1 and 2.

**Row 5:** Knit across.

**Row 6:** K1, P1, K1, (P3, K1) across to last 2 pegs, P1, K1.

**Rows 7 and 8:** Repeat Rows 5 and 6.

Repeat Rows 1-8 for pattern.

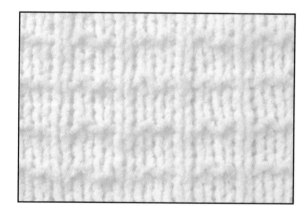

## #10 CHECKS STITCH

**Multiple:** 3 pegs

**Rows 1 and 2:** Knit across.

**Row 3:** K2, P2, (K1, P2) across to last 2 pegs, K2.

**Rows 4-6:** Knit across.

Repeat Rows 3-6 for pattern.

## #11 HARRIS TWEED RIB

**Multiple:** 4 + 1 pegs

**Row 1:** K3, P2, (K2, P2) across to last 4 pegs, K4.

**Row 2:** K4, P2, (K2, P2) across to last 3 pegs, K3.

**Rows 3 and 4:** Knit across.

**Row 5:** K3, P2, (K2, P2) across to last 4 pegs, K4.

**Row 6:** K4, P2, (K2, P2) across to last 3 pegs, K3.

**Rows 7 and 8:** K1, purl across to last peg, K1.

Repeat Rows 1-8 for pattern.

## #12 SEED STITCH CHECKS

**Multiple:** 10 + 7 pegs

**Row 1:** K6, P1, (K1, P1) twice, ★ K5, P1, (K1, P1) twice; repeat from ★ across to last 6 pegs, K6.

**Row 2:** K7, ★ P1, K1, P1, K7; repeat from ★ across.

**Rows 3-5:** Repeat Rows 1 and 2 once, then repeat Row 1 once **more**.

**Row 6:** (K1, P1) 3 times, K5, ★ P1, (K1, P1) twice, K5; repeat from ★ across to last 6 pegs, (P1, K1) 3 times.

**Row 7:** K2, P1, K1, P1, ★ K7, P1, K1, P1; repeat from ★ across to last 2 pegs, K2.

**Rows 8-10:** Repeat Rows 6 and 7 once, then repeat Row 6 once **more**.

Repeat Rows 1-10 for pattern.

## #13 GRID STITCH

**Multiple:** odd number of pegs

**Rows 1 and 2:** K2, P1, (K1, P1) across to last 2 pegs, K2.

**Row 3:** Knit across.

**Row 4:** K1, purl across to last peg, K1.

Repeat Rows 1-4 for pattern.

## #14 STROKES STITCH

**Multiple:** 11 + 4 pegs

**Row 1:** K2, P5, (K6, P5) across to last 8 pegs, K8.

**Row 2:** K8, P5, (K6, P5) across to last 2 pegs, K2.

**Rows 3 and 4:** Knit across.

**Row 5:** K8, P5, (K6, P5) across to last 2 pegs, K2.

**Row 6:** K2, P5, (K6, P5) across to last 8 pegs, K8.

**Rows 7 and 8:** Knit across.

Repeat Rows 1-8 for pattern.

## #15 WOVEN STITCH

**Multiple:** 4 pegs

**Rows 1 and 2:** Knit across.

**Rows 3 and 4:** K3, P2, (K2, P2) across to last 3 pegs, K3.

**Rows 5 and 6:** Knit across.

**Rows 7 and 8:** K1, P2, (K2, P2) across to last peg, K1.

Repeat Rows 1-8 for pattern.

## #16 MOSS STITCH CHECKERS

**Multiple:** 6 + 2 pegs

**Row 1:** (K5, P1) across to last 2 pegs, K2.

**Row 2:** (K1, P1) twice, (K3, P1, K1, P1) across to last 4 pegs, K4.

**Rows 3 and 4:** Repeat Rows 1 and 2.

**Row 5:** K2, (P1, K5) across.

**Row 6:** K4, P1, K1, P1, (K3, P1, K1, P1) across to last peg, K1.

**Rows 7 and 8:** Repeat Rows 5 and 6.

Repeat Rows 1-8 for pattern.

## #17 STAGGERED INTERRUPTED RIB

**Multiple:** 4 pegs

**Rows 1 and 2:** K3, P2, (K2, P2) across to last 3 pegs, K3.

**Row 3:** Knit across.

**Row 4:** K1, purl across to last peg, K1.

**Rows 5 and 6:** K1, P2, (K2, P2) across to last peg, K1.

**Row 7:** Knit across.

**Row 8:** K1, purl across to last peg, K1.

Repeat Rows 1-8 for pattern.

## #18 MOSS RIB

**Multiple:** 6 + 3 pegs

**Rows 1 and 2:** K1, (P1, K1) across.

**Rows 3 and 4:** K1, P1, (K2, P1) across to last peg, K1.

Repeat Rows 1-4 for pattern.

## #19 FLECK STITCH

**Multiple:** odd number of pegs

**Rows 1 and 2:** Knit across.

**Row 3:** K2, P1, (K1, P1) across to last 2 pegs, K2.

**Rows 4-6:** Knit across.

Repeat Rows 3-6 for pattern.

## #20 SEEDED RIB

**Multiple:** 6 + 3 pegs

**Row 1:** K3, (P1, K1, P1, K3) across.

**Row 2:** K4, P1, (K5, P1) across to last 4 pegs, K4.

Repeat Rows 1 and 2 for pattern.

## #21 DIAGONAL 4 LEFT

**Multiple:** 6 + 2 pegs

**Row 1:** K1, P2, (K4, P2) across to last 5 pegs, K5.

**Row 2:** K5, P2, (K4, P2) across to last peg, K1.

**Rows 3 and 4:** Repeat Rows 1 and 2.

**Rows 5-8:** K3, P2, (K4, P2) across to last 3 pegs, K3.

**Row 9:** K5, P2, (K4, P2) across to last peg, K1.

**Row 10:** K1, P2, (K4, P2) across to last 5 pegs, K5.

**Rows 11 and 12:** Repeat Rows 9 and 10.

Repeat Rows 1-12 for pattern.

## #22 FENCES STITCH

**Multiple:** 4 + 2 pegs

**Row 1:** K1, P2, (K2, P2) across to last 3 pegs, K3.

**Row 2:** K3, P2, (K2, P2) across to last peg, K1.

**Rows 3 and 4:** Repeat Rows 1 and 2.

**Row 5:** K1, purl across to last peg, K1.

**Row 6:** Knit across.

**Row 7:** K3, P2, (K2, P2) across to last peg, K1.

**Row 8:** K1, P2, (K2, P2) across to last 3 pegs, K3.

**Rows 9 and 10:** Repeat Rows 7 and 8.

**Row 11:** K1, purl across to last peg, K1.

**Row 12:** Knit across.

Repeat Rows 1-12 for pattern.

## #23 DIAGONAL 4 RIGHT

**Multiple:** 6 + 2 pegs

**Row 1:** K5, P2, (K4, P2) across to last peg, K1.

**Row 2:** K1, P2, (K4, P2) across to last 5 pegs, K5.

**Rows 3 and 4:** Repeat Rows 1 and 2.

**Rows 5-8:** K3, P2, (K4, P2) across to last 3 pegs, K3.

**Row 9:** K1, P2, (K4, P2) across to last 5 pegs, K5.

**Row 10:** K5, P2, (K4, P2) across to last peg, K1.

**Rows 11 and 12:** Repeat Rows 9 and 10.

Repeat Rows 1-12 for pattern.

## #24 DOUBLE ANDALUSIAN STITCH

**Multiple:** 3 pegs

**Rows 1-3:** Knit across.

**Row 4:** K2, P2, (K1, P2) across to last 2 pegs, K2.

Repeat Rows 1-4 for pattern.

## #25 NUBBY PATTERN

**Multiple:** odd number of pegs

**Rows 1-3:** K1, (P1, K1) across.

**Row 4:** K2, P1, (K1, P1) across to last 2 pegs, K2.

Repeat Rows 1-4 for pattern.

## #26 INTERRUPTED RIB

**Multiple:** odd number of pegs

**Rows 1 and 2:** K2, P1, (K1, P1) across to last 2 pegs, K2.

**Rows 3 and 4:** K1, purl across to last peg, K1.

Repeat Rows 1-4 for pattern.

## #27 LITTLE BOXES

**Multiple:** 3 + 2 pegs

**Rows 1 and 2:** Knit across.

**Rows 3 and 4:** K1, P1, K1, (P2, K1) across to last 2 pegs, P1, K1.

Repeat Rows 1-4 for pattern.

## #28 DOUBLE MOSS STITCH

**Multiple:** even number of pegs

**Row 1:** K2, (P1, K1) across.

**Rows 2 and 3:** (K1, P1) across to last 2 pegs, K2.

**Rows 4 and 5:** K2, (P1, K1) across.

Repeat Rows 2-5 for pattern.

## #29 RECTANGULAR CHECKS

**Multiple:** 6 + 2 pegs

**Row 1:** Knit across.

**Row 2:** K1, P3, (K3, P3) across to last 4 pegs, K4.

**Rows 3-12:** Repeat Rows 1 and 2, 5 times.

**Row 13:** Knit across.

**Row 14:** K4, P3, (K3, P3) across to last peg, K1.

**Rows 15-24:** Repeat Rows 13 and 14, 5 times.

Repeat Rows 1-24 for pattern.

# 4-STITCH CABLES

**CROSS 4 RIGHT** *(abbreviated C4R)*
  *(uses 4 pegs)*

Bring the working yarn behind the next 2 pegs, then back to the outside *(Fig. A)*.

Knit the next 2 pegs, then place them onto a cable needle *(Fig. B)* and let it hang at the inside of the loom.

Bring the working yarn behind all 4 pegs, then back to the outside before the first skipped peg *(Fig. C)*.

Knit the 2 skipped pegs, then use the tool to move them to the empty pegs, keeping them in the same order *(Fig. D)*.

Place the loops from the cable needle onto the new empty pegs, keeping them in the same order *(Fig. E)*.

> **TIP:** The stitches should always be worked loosely, allowing them to be easily moved. Once the cable stitches have been moved, take up the slack of each stitch by gently tugging on the yarn.

**CROSS 4 LEFT** *(abbreviated C4L)*
  *(uses 4 pegs)*

Place the loops from the next 2 pegs onto a cable needle and let it hang at the inside of the loom. Bring the working yarn behind the 2 empty pegs, then back to the outside *(Fig. F)*.

Knit the next 2 pegs, then use the tool to move them to the empty pegs, keeping them in the same order *(Fig. G)*. With the working yarn outside the loom, place the loops from the cable needle onto the new empty pegs, keeping them in the same order, and knit them. Take up the slack of each stitch by gently tugging on the yarn.

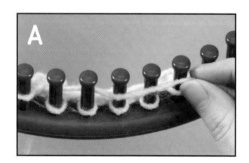

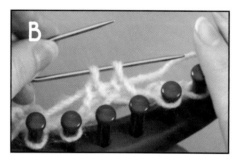

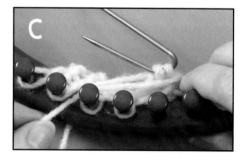

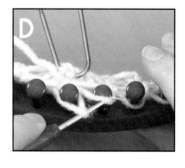

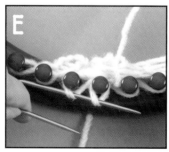

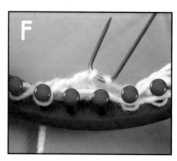

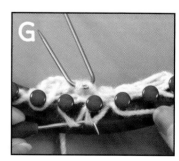

## #30 CORKSCREW CABLE

**Panel:** 14 pegs

See 4-Stitch Cables on page 24.

**Row 1:** Knit across.

**Row 2:** K3, P2, K4, P2, K3.

**Row 3:** Knit across.

**Row 4:** K3, P2, C4R, P2, K3.

**Rows 5-12:** Repeat Rows 1-4 twice.

**Rows 13-27:** Repeat Rows 1 and 2, 7 times, then repeat Row 1 once **more**.

Repeat Rows 4-27 for pattern.

## #31 ELONGATED WAVE CABLE

**Panel:** 14 pegs

See 4-Stitch Cables on page 24.

**Row 1:** K3, P2, K4, P2, K3.

**Row 2:** K3, P2, C4R, P2, K3.

**Rows 3-9:** K3, P2, K4, P2, K3.

**Row 10:** K3, P2, C4L, P2, K3.

**Rows 11-17:** K3, P2, K4, P2, K3.

Repeat Rows 2-17 for pattern.

## #32 LINKS CABLE

**Panel:** 16 pegs

See 4-Stitch Cables on page 24.

**Rows 1-3:** K1, P3, K2, P4, K2, P3, K1.

**Row 4:** K1, P3, C4R, C4L, P3, K1.

**Rows 5-11:** K1, P3, K2, P4, K2, P3, K1.

Repeat Rows 4-11 for pattern.

# 3-STITCH CABLES

Both of these 3-stitch cables are worked over a foundation of two knit stitches and one skipped stitch.

**To skip 1**, place the working yarn behind the next peg, leaving it unworked, then back to the outside **(Fig. H)**. Work the next peg keeping even tension on the working yarn.

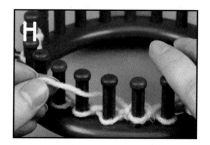

**CABLE 3 RIGHT** *(abbreviated C3R)* (uses 3 pegs)

Bring the working yarn behind the next peg, then back to the outside. Knit the next 2 pegs, then place them onto a cable needle and let it hang at the inside of the loom.

Bring the working yarn behind all 3 pegs, then back to the outside before the skipped peg. Knit the skipped peg, then use the tool to move it to the second empty peg. Place the loops from the cable needle onto the new empty pegs, keeping them in the same order.

**CABLE 3 LEFT** *(abbreviated C3L)* (uses 3 pegs)

Place the loops from the next 2 pegs onto a cable needle and let it hang at the inside of the loom. Bring the working yarn behind the empty pegs, then back to the outside. Knit the next peg, then use the tool to move it to the first empty peg. With the working yarn outside the loom, place the loops from the cable needle onto the new empty pegs, keeping them in the same order, and knit them. Take up the slack of each stitch by gently tugging on the yarn.

**TIP:** The stitches should always be worked **loosely**, allowing them to be easily moved. Once the cable stitches have been moved, take up the slack of each stitch by gently tugging on the yarn.

## #33 DOUBLE CABLE DOWNWARDS

**Panel:** 20 pegs

See 3-Stitch Cables on page 26.

**Row 1:** K4, P3, K6, P3, K4.

**Rows 2 and 3:** K4, P3, skip 1, K4, skip 1, P3, K4.

**Row 4:** K4, P3, C3R, C3L, P3, K4.

**Row 5:** K4, P3, K6, P3, K4.

**Rows 6-9:** K4, P3, skip 1, K4, skip 1, P3, K4.

Repeat Rows 4-9 for pattern.

## #34 DOUBLE CABLE UPWARDS

**Panel:** 20 pegs

See 3-Stitch Cables on page 26.

**Row 1:** K4, P3, K6, P3, K4.

**Rows 2 and 3:** K4, P3, K2, skip 2, K2, P3, K4.

**Row 4:** K4, P3, C3L, C3R, P3, K4.

**Row 5:** K4, P3, K6, P3, K4.

**Rows 6-9:** K4, P3, K2, skip 2, K2, P3, K4.

Repeat Rows 4-9 for pattern.

## #35 SLIPPED DOUBLE CHAIN

**Panel:** 16 pegs

See 3-Stitch Cables on page 26.

**Row 1:** K1, P3, K7, P3, K2.

**Row 2:** K2, P3, skip 1, K5, skip 1, P3, K1.

**Row 3:** K1, P3, skip 1, K5, skip 1, P3, K2.

**Row 4:** K2, P3, C3R, K1, C3L, P3, K1.

**Row 5:** K1, P3, K7, P3, K2.

**Row 6:** K2, P3, K2, skip 1, K1, skip 1, K2, P3, K1.

**Row 7:** K1, P3, K2, skip 1, K1, skip 1, K2, P3, K2.

**Row 8:** K2, P3, C3L, K1, C3R, P3, K1.

Repeat Rows 1-8 for pattern.

# GENERAL INSTRUCTIONS

## ABBREVIATIONS

| | |
|---|---|
| cm | centimeters |
| C3L | cable 3 left |
| C3R | cable 3 right |
| C4L | cross 4 left |
| C4R | cross 4 right |
| K | knit |
| mm | millimeters |
| P | purl |

## SYMBOLS & TERMS

★ — work instructions following ★ as many **more** times as indicated in addition to the first time.

( ) or [ ] — work enclosed instructions **as many** times as specified by the number immediately following **or** contains explanatory remarks.

## GAUGE

Gauge is the number of stitches and rows in every inch of your knitting and is used to control the finished size.

Exact gauge is essential for proper size. Before beginning your project, make a sample swatch approximately 4" (10 cm) wide with the yarn and loom specified in the individual instructions. After completing the swatch, give it a tug, holding the cast on and bound off edges, then let it "rest".

Measure it, counting your stitches and rows carefully. If your swatch is larger or smaller than specified, make another, changing your tension of the working yarn as you form the stitches. Keep trying until you find the tension you need to achieve gauge. Maintain established gauge throughout project.

## WEAVING SEAMS

With the **right** side of both pieces facing you and edges even, sew through both sides once to secure the seam. Insert the needle under the bar between the first and second stitches on the row and pull the yarn through *(Fig. 1)*. Insert the needle under the next bar on the second side. Repeat from side to side, being careful to match rows. If the edges are different lengths, it may be necessary to insert the needle under two bars at one edge.

**Fig. 1**

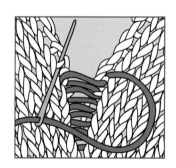

## WORKSHEETS

Use the worksheets on pages 29-31 to plan your own samplers. On each strip, fill in the following information:

Pattern stitch(es)

Width of strip

Number of stitches

Multiple

Color (if more than one)

| Yarn Weight Symbol & Names | SUPER FINE 1 | FINE 2 | LIGHT 3 | MEDIUM 4 | BULKY 5 | SUPER BULKY 6 | JUMBO 7 |
|---|---|---|---|---|---|---|---|
| Type of Yarns in Category | Sock, Fingering, Baby | Sport, Baby | DK, Light Worsted | Worsted, Afghan, Aran | Chunky, Craft, Rug | Bulky, Roving | Jumbo, Roving |

| | |
|---|---|
| ◼◻◻◻ **BEGINNER** | Projects for first-time loom knitters using basic knit and purl stitches, and simple color changes. |
| ◼◼◻◻ **EASY** | Projects using basic stitches, repetitive stitch patterns, simple color changes, and simple shaping and finishing. |
| ◼◼◻◻ **EASY +** | Projects using basic stitches, repetitive stitch patterns, simple color changes, simple short rows, and simple shaping and finishing. |
| ◼◼◼◻ **INTERMEDIATE** | Projects with a variety of stitches, such as lace, also short rows, and mid-level shaping and finishing. |

# 5-Strip Worksheet

See Worksheets, page 28.

1. Yarn: _____

2. Loom: _____

3. Gauge: _____

4. Finished Size: _____

| Strip 1 | Strip 2 | Strip 3 | Strip 4 | Strip 5 |
|---------|---------|---------|---------|---------|
|         |         |         |         |         |

↑ **Working direction**

# 12-Block Worksheet

See Worksheets, page 28.

1. Yarn: _____

2. Loom: _____

3. Gauge: _____

4. Finished Size: _____

| Strip 1 | Strip 2 | Strip 3 | Strip 4 |
|---------|---------|---------|---------|
|         |         |         |         |
|         |         |         |         |
|         |         |         |         |

↑ **Working direction**

# 7-Strip Worksheet

See Worksheets, page 28.

1. Yarn: _____

2. Loom: _____

3. Gauge: _____

4. Finished Size: _____

Strip 7

Strip 6

Strip 5

Strip 4

Strip 3

Strip 2

Strip 1

→ **Working direction**

## YARN INFORMATION

The items in this book were made using a variety of yarns. Any brand of the specified weight of yarn may be used. It is best to refer to the yardage/meters when determining how many skeins or balls to purchase. Remember, to arrive at the finished size, it is the GAUGE/TENSION that is important, not the brand of yarn.

For your convenience, listed below are the yarns used to create our photography models. Because yarn manufacturers make frequent changes in their product lines, you may sometimes find it necessary to use a substitute yarn or to search for the discontinued product at alternate suppliers (locally or online).

### LAP-GHAN

*Lion Brand® Heartland®*
#305 Glacier Bay Tweed

### BABY-GHAN

*Red Heart® Cutie Pie™*
Grey - #419 Koala
White - #10 Cotton

### AFGHAN

*Lion Brand® Wool-Ease®*
*Thick & Quick®*
#151 Graphite

# MEET KATHY NORRIS

Like most people, Kathy Norris learned to knit in the traditional style, using knitting needles. She discovered loom knitting at the craft supply store where she worked in Southern California. She says, "They handed me a knitting loom and told me to figure it out. So I taught myself how to use it."

Kathy used her first loom knitting designs to teach others the fun new skill. In 2005, she began publishing her patterns. "I was attracted to loom knitting because, as a designer, you have to find a new way to work with the geometry of knitting. Once you have the loom knitting basics down, you can start experimenting to make the loom do what you want."

For additional stitch patterns to knit with looms of all sizes and shapes, including Leisure Arts oval looms, look for Kathy's *Loom Knit Stitch Dictionary* (#75566).

Other Leisure Arts books and ebooks featuring Kathy's designs include *Oval Loom Knit Collection* (#6888), *Loom Knit Baby Wraps* (#6667), *Big Book of Loom Knit Cowls* (#6611), *Loom Knit Dishcloths* (#6369), *Loom Knit Hats & Scarves* (#75471), *More Knitting Wheel Fashions* (#4411), *I Can't Believe I'm Loom Knitting* (#5250), *Big Book of Loom Knitting* (#5604), and *Loom Knitting for Mommy & Me* (#5942). For more about Kathy, visit KathyNorrisDesigns.com.

We have made every effort to ensure that these instructions are accurate and complete. We cannot, however, be responsible for human error, typographical mistakes, or variations in individual work.

Production Team: Instructional/Technical Writer - Cathy Hardy; Editorial Writer - Susan Frantz Wiles; Senior Graphic Artist - Lora Puls; Graphic Artist - Victoria Temple; Photo Stylist - Lori Wenger; and Photographer - Jason Masters.

Lap-ghan instructions were tested and photo model was made by Nancy Desmarais.